he Origin of the War Term "No Man's Land" as Applied to the World War

OF THE

DIETRICK FAMILY OF HOLLAND

The deep red background of the shield exhibits the honor and distinction won for the family by its members who participated in the crusades, for at the time no families were permitted to display red on their arms unless representatives of the house had seen service in the wars for the recovery of the sacred places in Palestine. The stars suggest the loftiness of aim and the ambition of the bearers of the arms. The wing like leaves or side ornaments on the sides, symbolize the virtue and valor which arise above all that is unworthy and upbear the shield as on angels wings towards the stars above.

The silver and gold typify the untarnished honor of the family, while the blue indicates the fidelity and loyalty of the owners of this insignia to the cause which they espoused and the overlords to whom they had vowed allegiance. The green, beneath the cross, agrees with the springtime of life and the flower of manhood who bore this symbol, the freshest and choicest part of an army, and signifies youth, hope and progress. The peacock feathers surmounting the crest of the helmet set forth the dignity of the house and the proper pride which its members felt in the achievements of their doughty ancestors. The golden stars inlaid indicate that this self complacency is justifiable and that no stain has marred the dignity of the house.

AD FINEM FIDELIS—*Faithful to the end*

The Origin of the War Term

"No Man's Land"

As Applied to the World War

BY

J. HOWARD RANDERSON

Former member of the 220th and 668th Aero Squadrons, U. S.
Army, member of the New England Historical and Geneological
Society, Albany Institute and Historical and Art Society,
University Club of Albany, Lake George Country Club,
Lake Placid Club, Colonnade Club of Virginia,
Society of the Sons of the Revolution, the
American Legion, and the Dartmouth
Alumni Association

Originator of the War Terms:—

"No Man's Land"; a battlefield in the World War.

"Over the top"; an expression used in the trenches.

"Buddy"; a name used in the army and navy for companion
   or mate, also an authorized greeting among members
   of the American Legion.

"Gob"; a name for sailor in the navy.

Also the following humorous expressions which were in
   general use during the time of the World War, and
   which were current in the army and navy –

"Let's go."

"I'll tell the World."

"You said a mouthful."

"It's a great life if you don't weaken."

"You drive and I'll shovel."

"A man may be down, but he's never out"; a slogan adopted
   during the World War by the Salvation Army and also
   by the 5th Liberty Loan Campaign.

And many others.

———

Also originator, and a founder, of the Dartmouth "Jack
   O'Lantern,"—the Dartmouth College Humorous Maga-
   zine.

PROLOGUE

The subject matter of the following pages was drawn primarily from the author's experiences which began on an island in Lake Champlain near Westport, New York, called No Man's Island, and his subsequent discussions with a group of distinguished gentlemen, the majority of whom were foreign personages, and I might say, leaders of thought and philanthropy in Europe. Among these was the late Count Casimir de Monkowski, owner of the famous motor boat, the "Ankle Deep", which won many speed championships on the St. Lawrence River and Lake George during the last decade.

The time Mr. Randerson spent on the above mentioned island covered a period of several summers which dates back to over twenty years ago, in his early boyhood. The extreme loneliness, the awful isolation of the island, impressed him as a veritable, No Man's Island, for it seemed to him as if every living thing shunned it, and it remained there secluded and unseen, year after year, the days and months passing, without its existence being noted by those to whom time had a meaning, except to himself, and a few others, attracted to it by its very barrenness and abandonment. It was this island that inspired Mr. Randerson afterwards with the name "No Man's Land", for it was analogous in many respects, and possessed many of the vivid settings and elements of the "No Man's Land" of the World War. The semblance was startling,—with the exception of the destruction wrought by the fearful mechanism of modern warfare in the case of "No Man's Land" of Europe.

However, in 1914, when the German Army was crushing its way forward with deliberate and wanton vandalism against the allied nations, and its cruel indignities and horrorable possibilities were being discussed in their various aspects by Mr. Randerson and a group of noblemen who were at Lake George at that time, the term "No Man's Land" suggested itself to him, by a turn of the mind which carried him back to the lonely and desolate island in Lake Champlain, and then overseas to the region and places where lonesomeness and desolation were the product, not of nature, as was the case of the island, but the diabolical and infernal ingenuity of man.

Specifically, the actaul instance of Mr. Randerson's first using the term "No Man's Land" is as follows:

He was asked, during a conversation with the aforesaid noblemen, what his opinion was of the war. This was at the time when the Germans were raging havoc in Belgium and France not many weeks after the war had begun. The territory through which they were advancing was once the land of Mr. Randerson's ancestors. His reply was significant and emphatic;—namely, that they were in the act of making a "No Man's Land" out of Europe. The term impressed these noblemen, who were owners of vast estates in Europe, to such a degree that immediate steps were taken to make every possible and conceivable effort to prevent further or absolute destruction. Soon afterwards the expression was adopted by them as a name for a battle area in the World war. It was through Mr. Randerson's connections here in this country that the name was brought into use in America.

In addition to having originated the term "No Man's Land", the following expressions, destined later to be popularized and hallowed by their usage in the World War, were originated on board a ship sailing from New Orleans to New York in December, 1916, when Mr. Randerson was returning to his home following an extended trip through the western states. Aboard this ship were many soldiers, members of various military organizations from different cities in the United States. Most of them were returning home on leave of absence from the Mexican border. It was at the time we were in the midst of our prolonged trouble with Mexico, a situation which necessitated the patrolling of the border by the National Guard and other troops.

Soon after leaving New Orleans, trouble arose among the men. A soldier was accused by his comrades of a serious offense. A committee of investigation was appointed, and a court constituted by soldiers and officers, tried the offender. The situation became serious and intense.* Excitement ran high, and the emotions of those aboard, seeking an outlet, were manifested by the expressions which became so widely current later, and which were born at that time. Such idioms of the trenches as, "I'll tell the world", "How do you get that way", "Where do you get that stuff", and others less striking, perhaps, and therefore less familiar, were then used, I believe, for the first time. They were the product of excitement and trouble which prevailed among the men aboard the ship. And what a usage they enjoyed in the army later! With the slang thus added to the military vernacular were also created the titles of many songs afterward popular among the soldiery, "Pack all your troubles in your old kit bag", "Where do we go from here" "When the clouds in the sky roll by", and others. The expression, "It's a great life if you don't weaken" was brought into fame on this

*It was through the efforts of Mr. Randerson, and another man, that this unpleasant affair was brought to a satisfactory conclusion. The newspapers at the time acclaimed it as one of the most chivalrous deeds in recent history.

voyage although it was originated by Mr. Randerson in Seattle, Washington, several weeks previous to that time. Also a host of similar phrases sprung up on this ship which do not here readily suggest themselves; all of which impressed those who heard them to a point where they speedily went the rounds of the ship and thence were imported into New York and later into the great armies of the Allies. There is no question that the battery of expressions, so created, however whimsical and slangy some of them may have seemed to the public as a whole, after having adjusted themselves properly to suit the peculiarities, caprices and exigencies of the life in the trenches, added considerably to the spirit and morale of the men in their days of struggle and hardship.

Another matter of note which resulted from Mr. Randerson's visit to Lake George in the summer of 1914 was his mentioning the similarity between the allied nations as they entered the World War and the ancient apologue entitled, "The Fagot of Sticks". Perhaps the reader will recall the story. Mr. Randerson related it to the group of nobleman, to whom reference was made in a preceeding paragraph, suggesting its application to the European situation on the allied side, and they praised the accuracy of the comparison. The fable, in the connection to which Mr. Randerson assigned it, was afterward related abroad at a critical point in the war, by one of the noblemen of the Lake George group. Thereafter it was very frequently quoted as a similitude for the war situation. It is related on excellent authority that the late Czar Nicholas of Russia so used it. The fable, roughly narrated from memory, runs as follows:

An old man on the point of death, summoned his sons around him to give them some parting advice. He ordered his servant to bring in a bundle of sticks, bound firmly together, and said to his oldest son, "Break them!" The son strained and strained, but with all his efforts was unable to break the bundle. The other sons also tried, but none of them were successful. "Untie the bundle," said the father, "and each of you take a stick." When they had done so, he called out to them, "Now break", and each stick was easily broken. "You see my meaning", said the father. "If you stand together no one can break you." So it was with the Allies! Bound together in the common cause, united for the realization of a humane and practical ideal, no German military idea of the will to conquer, or dominate, could prevail against them.

During the course of Mr. Randerson's life, his acquaintance with the afore-mentioned noblemen, many of them representing the most notable families in Europe, has been kindled and ripened into friendship through incidents and occasional meetings which have occurred in this country and abroad, as well as through his ancestral connections. Mr. Randerson is a descendant of prominent and noted American ancestry who distinguished themselves in the history and development of this country. Among these are John Howland who came to this country on the "Mayflower" landing with the Pilgrims in 1620; Dr. James Noyes, of Harvard University, one of the founders and first trustees of Yale University; and Captain William and Colonel Joseph Champlain of the Continental Army. He is also of noble English, French and Dutch ancestry which extends back to William the Conqueror, Duke of Normandy, through Edward III, King of England, the Lakes of Normantown and the Howard family of Yorkshire; also Theodoric the Great, King of the Goths and Romans through the Dietrick family of Holland; and the right line of Charlemagne through Louis IV, King of France, the Dukes of Lorraine and Louvaine, Counts of Luxemburg, Namur and Mons, and the Earls of Arundel and Sussex.

The Coat of Arms of the Dietrick family is reproduced on a preceding page.

New York, N. Y., U. S. A.,   L. H. C.
    December, 1922.

---

*The name "No Man's Land" was later applied to the Bad Lands and parts of the unproductive regions of Arizona and the great southwest, following a motor trip through that region by Mr. Randerson.

[8]

THE ORIGIN OF THE WAR TERM—"NO MAN'S LAND."

THE ORIGIN OF THE WAR TERM "NO MAN'S LAND"

BY

J. HOWARD RANDERSON

N that region of the World beyond the Atlantic, ever so far remote from us, surrounded by pleasant valleys and vineyards, in the northern part of Europe, lies a devastated territory which was once called "No Man's Land". True this land was once the scene of terrible conflict where horror and desolation reigned for more than four long years. It is now shrouded with a cloak of sanctity and deep mourning for those who fought and gave their lives there that civilization might live.

It has been requested of me to relate the history of the term "No Man's Land", from the time I first mentioned it during the early days of the World War when the Germans were invading Belgium and France to end their forward career at the Marne a few weeks later. While I am by no means certain that anything I might say will be worthy of a place among the eloquent tributes that have been heretofore written, I have sought to do what seemed to me most essential,—that is, to give a brief, truthful and at the same time descriptive presentation of the origin of this signally important term which was conspicuous during the war, and which, I believe, has found a sacred place in the hearts and memories of those who were in any way connected with the war.

I was at Lake George in the State of New York in the late summer of 1914, when the German army was at the high tide of its fearful career through Belgium and France. The newspapers at the time were depicting, under startling headlines, men being torn to pieces, not singly, but in whole regiments, towns and farm lands being burned and destroyed, unheard-of cruelties inflicted upon the inhabitants, inhuman treatment of prisoners. The very conception of it all was rejected by the civilized mind as too fantastical and unreal. First we read of the Germans invading Luxemburg, then how they overran Belgium; then of Liege being occupied, then Brussels, Namur, the battle of Tannenberg, the destruction of Louvain, and how the British were swept down in the fields of Flanders in whole regiments and their entire army in France wiped out almost to the last battalion. How they, the Germans, forced the French line back to within a short distance of the very gates of Paris, where followed the

[11]

memorable battle of the Marne which ended the German advance and marked a crisis and turning point in the war, which was the beginning of a long gruelling counteraction of events and circumstances. It all came so suddenly, so unexpectedly, and appeared so foreign and remote at the time, that it seemed beyond human comprehension.

It was on account of these unheard of happenings, these inconceivable atrocities and horrors, which the Germans perpetrated in the first flush of their campaign of frightfulness, that I remarked, on a day soon after the war had begun, that they were making out of the territory over which they were raging warfare,—a no man's land, for it seemed to me that the land became, as the Germans forced their way into Belgium and France against the newly formed armies of the Allies, a region so thoroughly bereft and deprived of life that no living thing could exist there.

The term "No Man's Land" impressed a group of foreign noblemen, who were at Lake George at the time, as a very expressive and appropriate description, and it was through this group, whose members were in sympathy with the allies, that the phrase was adopted.

They carried it abroad. It became known in England, and then in France, and was circulated there through agencies associated with the members of the group of which I have spoken. Meanwhile the same expression was brought into use in this country as a result of my connection with newspapers at the time, and through conversation and correspondence. Thus it circulated in this country and abroad simultaneously, and within a remarkably short time, came into general use, not a descriptive applying to all the territory through which the Germans had advanced, but as a name for that stretch of land extending between the two opposing forces; or the territory lying directly between the first line trenches of the Allies and the Germans.

As the one through whom the expression "No Man's Land" came into use, I have, not unnaturally, pondered deeply upon it. I have considered the term in its practical as well as psychological aspects, in its relation to the morale of the soldiers. How did it affect their spirit; their will to victory? What it did, in fact, was to stimulate them; to urge them on to raise a means of protection and revolt against further oppression and destruction, to recover themselves as quickly as possible from the tremendous onslaught of the enemy and to carry on a crusade of justice and rightfulness against all future encroachments and barbarism, lest the whole World become a "No Man's Land" and a place unfit to live in. And also, equally important, the term symbolized CAUTION on the part of the men. History tells us that in previous wars, notably in our own Civil War, men unnecessarily and carelessly exposed themselves to danger and were consequently shot down in countless numbers, and it is for this reason that the name "No Man's Land" was needed as a symbol, a cabalistic sign that meant a warning— DANGER AHEAD!! PERIL!! KEEP OUT!!

Caution, which is one of first rules in discipline, was inspired by the term "No Man's Land". It kept men back. It made them careful. It advised them in unmistakable terms not to enter upon the territory which it was intended to name, unless under orders. To disregard its advise meant, of necessity, DEATH. The instruments of modern warfare were too terrible, too searching, too precise in their ability to reach their mark. Thus the warning could not, consistently with the instinct of self-preservation, be disregarded. Men who were in the front line trenches have said repeatedly that the temptation to go beyond, to venture OUT THERE, was extremely great. But the symbolic term "No Man's Land" operated with psychological exactitude. It counseled them not to go except when the exigencies of war demanded. The symbol "No Man's Land" was not employed in one sector alone. It was the prevailing signal of caution along the entire front,—in France, in Belgium, in Alsace, even in Poland and along the Isonzo on the Italian front, and in far off Mesopotamia and along the Dardanelles. Wherever troops used the English language they employed the term "No Man's Land."

There is scarcely a person who lived during the period of the World War who does not recall the harrowing stories which gravitated out of those battle areas, especially when they were being swept by heavy artillery and machine gun fire, to say nothing of the uncivilized uses of poison gas and other forbidden weapons of warfare. Verdun, the Marne, Chateau-Thierry, St. Mihiel, the Argonne Forest, the Chemin des Dames, St. Quentin, and other names, have been immortalized by their sinister significance in the greatest of all conflicts. Molested and destroyed nearly to extinction and almost beyond hope of eventual recovery, honey-combed and shell-pitted by mines and other high explosives, left destitute of all semblance of vegetation and life,— there remained a barren territory, many parts of which were underlaid with unexploded mines; unlivable,—unspeakable, where no man dared trespass.

It was a terrible gulf between the two opposing forces which seemed to swallow up all things human, which existed in so accurate a similitude of the inferno, as to surpass in reality any fantasy that has ever found its way into the human imagination.

Such, then, was "No Man's Land". Never in the history of the World has a place existed which bore so much suffering and hardship, such a multitude of death and horror, in a unit of area, as in this territory, which moved back and forth

[13]

with the fortunes of battle, and bore always the implied inscription,—"No Man's Land". The grief of a civilized world has proven how deep is the appreciation, how unstinted the thankfulness, which the World feels toward those men who gave their lives there that civilization might live, and the most beautiful and sacred tribute we can pay those men remains unspoken.

Since the war civilization has regarded "No Man's Land" with a new solemnity of remembrance and gratitude, because "No Man's Land" has acquired a meaning which will inhere in it to the end of time, inborn and inseparable to the World War. It is the meaning which the great and unselfish loyalty, the noble courage, the self-sacrificing heroism, of the men who fought and died there have given it. It was consecrated in their blood, and received the immortal title to survive after everything fashioned by human hands shall have passed away, the name of "No Man's Land".